From Distress
To Success!

RESTORATION OF THE BREACH
WITHOUT BORDERS

West Palm Beach, Florida

Rev. Dr. Francis J. Ford

ISBN: 978-1-954755-12-3

Published by:
Restoration of the Breach without Borders
133 45th Street, Building A7
West Palm Beach, Florida 33407
restorativeauthor@gmail.com
Tele: (561) 388-2949

EBook Cover Design by:
Calbert Simson
divine.creativevillage@gmail.com

Editing done by: Juan Pablo
juanpablo_20@hotmail.com

Formatting and Publishing done by:
Sherene Morrison
Publisher.20@aol.com

Unless otherwise stated Scripture verses are quoted from the King James Version of the Bible.

TABLE OF CONTENTS

DEDICATION

To my mother Minnie Johnson Ford (deceased), I never had enough time with you, but the few years you spent with us, you introduced us to Christ, even through pain, tears and fear. Mom, I can never thank you enough.

To my "Joy" Elmarie Ford, the one who keeps me going with positive thoughts, my best friend, confidant, and biggest supporter in all I do. You make my life complete.

To all my brothers Charles, Howard, Spaulding, Albert, and Curtis. To all my sisters Bertha Woodland, Gloria Speed, Sally Thomas, and Elder Evelyn Berry. To my children Angie, Kontina, Sierra,Walter, Devon and Gregory and to our youngest sons Miguel and Oshae Johnson, you both make me so proud to be called your dad. To my cousin Deacon Francis I Ford.

To God be the glory, who has blessed me through the years so that I could be a blessing to others along the way.

ACKNOWLEDGEMENTS

To The Triune God, my Primary Helper. I thank God for choosing me to live the life package which includes poverty and cancer with a healing deliverance.

Thanks, and appreciation to all my children and friends. They have been a tower of strength to me as I journeyed through being diagnosed, surgery and recovery. I love them dearly.

To my Joy, her sisters, especially Dolvis Parkes. To my praying mother-in-law, Mrs. Pauline Phipps, who treats me as nothing less than a real son. To my sisters, brothers and their children who gave incalculable support throughout my journey with cancer and back surgery I thank you sincerely.

Deacon Francis I. Ford, you have been a true encouragement to me. Your constant prayers have not gone unanswered.

Rev. Carl V. Messiah you have never forsaken me. You have been there through the good and the bad. I appreciate you.

My very good friend Rev. Lowell Hancock. You will forever be in my prayers. God used you to be my support in my early years of ministry.

My church family; Woodland Village Missionary Baptist Church, Mount Hope Missionary Baptist Church, Smith Chapel United Methodist Church, thank you for your continued support. You are a blessing to me.

To those who contributed to my life in one way or another whose names I did not identify, please know that you are not forgotten. I love you all sincerely.

Thanks, and appreciation Rev.Dr. Lanier Twyman and Rev. Dr. Sterling Swann for your endorsements.

I personally thank Bishop Timothy Warren for writing the foreword for my book From Distress To success.

INTRODUCTION

The limitations presented to you at birth are limited within themselves and can easily be the determining factors of your failures. Failures are easily the fruit of limitations, however, if you begin to see your challenges as the inspirations that God divinely reserved for you in propelling your greatness, success will be the new offspring of the said limitations.

Success is greatly appreciated when it is achieved amidst failures where family, friends and society's standards render you a failure before you consciously commenced the journey of living. Dr. Ford's success is a true testimony of going against the tides of present failures to achievement at levels where those who lacked confidence in him, are yet to mimic.

Dr. Ford's greatest achievement is yet to be accomplished, which is attainable but might be associated with great challenges. As you delve into his life's journey, his desire is for you to partner with him in attaining one more success- **Your Success.** Let his life *From Distress to Success* inspire and motivate you to be intentional and committed to achieving all that God has prepared for you. Start believing in yourself again or at higher levels. Readers, as you read, begin to envision your success and never lose sight of that vision.

ENDORSEMENTS

Masterfully, Rev. Dr. Francis J. Ford draws you into his life, from the trials and tribulations of early and adolescent childhood; the failures and hardships that he had to endure, to the victorious life he experienced in his later years. By an unswerving trust in God, he displays the faith necessary to endure and move from the distresses of the past to successes of the present. A must-read for the person struggling to persevere in this life.

-Rev. Dr. Sterling R. Swann, Jr., D.D., Th.D., Ed.D.
Pastor, Mt. Hope Missionary Baptist Church, Nanjemoy, Maryland
President, Wilbur H. Waters School of Religion, Inc. and Theological Seminary

* * * * *

Pastor Francis Ford has written a compelling book outlining his journey from tragedy to triumph. This reading provides hope and encouragement.

It speaks to all of us to endure hardships and continue moving forward.

-Bishop Lanier C. Twyman, Pastor
St. Stephen Baptist Church, Temple
Hills, Maryland

* * * * *

Rev. Dr. Francis Ford life's journey is one that is compact with the relevant tools to propel anyone to not settle for average or mediocre. Your early days of distress do not have to be the ending of your story. If you partner with God like Dr. Ford, God will change your story.

-Rev. Leostone Morrison
Author/Pastor

FOREWORD

I am honored to have this opportunity to write this Foreword for Rev. Dr. Francis Ford. He and his family have been a part of my life for over 44 years. He was a Deacon, Minister and my Sunday School Teacher at my father's church growing up. I've had a front row seat watching his Ministry unfold from his appointment to Deaconship to becoming the Pastor of the Oldest African American Congregation in Charles County, Maryland, The Mount Hope Missionary Baptist Church. I witnessed his initial Sermon as a boy at my father's church and was there for his final sermon as the Pastor at the Mt. Hope M.B. Church.

"...with God your victory is guaranteed. You will have good success because the victory is already won. What is required of you is to walk in perpetual victory."

From Distress to Success is a must read. This book is both informative and inspiring with its historical approach and exploration of his personal journey with God. The clear and vivid descriptions allow the reader to enter the experience. This book demonstrates for us that the hand of the Lord is in every aspect of our lives. Each chapter allows the reader to understand the power of God's love and care in the life of mankind. This book will leave you encouraged and assured that there is VICTORY in Jesus Christ. Be blessed, be edified.

-Bishop Timothy J. Warren
Pastor
The Holy Sanctuary
Waldorf, Maryland

CHAPTER 1
ROOTS

Pisgah, situated in the state of Maryland, was a very small town, with one grocery store, two gas stations, a post office and no streetlights. The little shack (House) I was raised in had three bedrooms, a kitchen, a living room and a large porch which was later converted into two additional rooms as the family grew. My mother, Minnie G. Johnson Ford was a stay at home wife with thirteen children of which I am the second oldest, but the first for my father, Francis I. Ford. He never allowed his beautiful wife to seek employment. I was born on July 4th, 1944; and was named Francis Joseph Ford after my father. My Twelve siblings in order are, Thomas (the eldest; deceased) Charles, Roman (deceased) Howard, Bertha, Minnie (deceased) Gloria, Maggie, Spaulding, Albert, Evenlyn, and Curtis.

Growing up we had no electricity, water, or bathroom. Our source of lighting was our kerosene lamps with the words *Home Sweet Home* written on the lamp shade. We only had two to supply the house, and at bedtime one was placed in the kitchen, turned down real low and burned throughout the night. We had to complete all our assignments and chores before it got dark. For water, we had to fetch water from the well which was about two hundred and twenty yards away from the house. Water buckets were used to transport the precious commodity. These buckets were carried by hand. For showering, especially during the summer, water was fetched and poured into a tin tub. This was allowed to sit in the sun for heating. During the winter we used foot tubs and basins; during this period water was heated on the stove.

We had two stoves: a cast iron which was used for cooking, and a tin heater which was used for heating the house. Both used wood fire. Our home sat on Eleven and a half acres of land covered with trees. An axe or a crosscut saw were the tools of choice used in cutting the much needed firewood. As nature requires that we relieve ourselves, an outside toilet was made. This was a hole dug in the ground about 3 by 3 square ft., with a seat built over it. Privacy while doing our duty was provided by a rustic wooden enclosure fitted with a door. This was located about ten yards from the house. Whenever it got full, we would close it and dig another one. The newspapers and regular brown paper that we used for cleaning ourselves after each usage increased the speed at which each hole was filled.

My mother's angelic personality saw her being quiet, soft spoken, and compassionate. She was brown skinned, medium built, and had short hair; She was about 5ft 5" and weighed about 225 lbs. My sister Bertha, who we call Polly, looks just like her.

My mom was known for the best homemade biscuits in town. Everyone came for those biscuits. Her favourite meal was fried chicken, mashed potatoes, gravy and kale. She would use the back and neck portions of the chicken to make the gravy for the mashed potatoes, and it was delicious. She was not just the cook, but also the disciplinarian of the household. Discipline was mostly administered using a switch; a flexible tree shoot. She would send the child or children to be disciplined to the woods to get the switch. If it was too thin, she would send you back until you came with an appropriate one.

My mom was also fond of singing. I fondly remember her singing, *"Mother's little children see a hard time when the mother is gone, nowhere to run, nowhere to go, only run from door to door."* She also sang the hymn, *"If I could hear my mother pray again."* (When my mother was alive, she took me to church, taught me from the bible how to sing and pray. But now she is gone and resting around the throne; if I

4

could only hear my mother pray again). Now looking back, she was always singing sad songs. Maybe this was due to her missing her mother who died when I was about Four years old. I spent a lot of time sitting on the kitchen floor watching my mother cook and listening to her beautiful voice saturate the atmosphere. She sang while cooking and after meals. Having spent a lot of time around her, I subsequently learned how to cook and comb my sisters' hair.

My mother knew the Lord but did not get the opportunity to attend her church regularly.

However, she never missed the funeral services of her kinfolks. She was Baptist and her home church was Oak Grove Baptist church in Nanjemoy. This was a long distance away from home and we lacked transportation. However, she made sure to send us, the children, to a nearby church every Sunday where Mrs. Alice Brown had attended before she died. Mrs. Alice was a neighbour, who was like an angel. We attended Smith Chapel United Methodists Church in Pisgah Maryland. Mrs. Amilla and her husband Mr. Robert Brown, both Sunday school teachers, were very good to us. They took us under their protection and treated us as though we were their very own. Mr. Brown was also a trustee at the church.

I was born with one leg; my right leg never grew. So, I have a short stomp below the knee. The toes on my right foot grew to a certain size then fell off. What should have been toes, seemed like little potatoes protruding from my knee. One day my brother Roman found one in the bed and thought it was an actual potato. I had surgery for this condition when I was about the age of Five years old. Growing up among my siblings and being the only one with a disability, I felt as though I was cheated of the basic things that a child does, like running. It is still a desire or dream of mine at the age of Seventy Six years old to experience the ability to run.

Mr. Sam Briscoe, another neighbor, made me a crutch. Before this, I got around, by crawling on my hands and knees. The crutch looked very similar to a regular crutch although it was made from small thin trees, held together by nails. I was very happy and proud of it because it was something that helped me to be mobile and helped a lot with ambulation.

I felt as though I had to compete to prove that I could be as good as my brothers and sisters. My siblings showed me respect and treated me like a big brother. They listened when I spoke. However, there were disagreements at times, especially between Thomas and I. We settled disputes between brothers by fighting outside. And despite my disability, I was a good fighter (with my prosthesis on). I was also fascinated with bodybuilding. The lack of a gym did not discourage me; I did push-ups and for weighted exercises I improvised using readily available materials in the woods such as heavy rocks. The results of my work-outs were noticeable as I developed big muscles and a broad chest.

Mrs. Madeleine Butler, the principal and a teacher at Mason Spring Elementary school partnered with Mr. Genome (Jerome) Swann and his wife, Theresa, who owned the grocery store in our community, in order to provide transportation for my medical visits. Those visits were necessary as I was being prepared to receive a prosthetic leg. They transported my mother, father, and myself back and forth for a penny a mile to Johns Hopkins Hospital in Baltimore, which was approximately between Forty Nine to Fifty-Five miles away from home. Before the prosthetic leg could be made, I had to do several tests and one surgery. These tests were done to ascertain the shape and the exact location of the bones. And surgery was done to remove the potato looking toes, and to shape my knee into a round shape.

I spent approximately Eight or Nine months in the hospital, but sadly, it felt much longer. It took quite some time for me to get used to being away from my parents and siblings. My parents were poor and never had their own transportation, so they could only afford to come see me every other week. When they came, they would bring me apples, oranges, and chewing gum. I would be so happy to see them, but unfortunately their visits were very short. Though I understood why they had to leave; I would always feel a sense of despair after they left. A prosthetic leg was made for my right foot during my hospital stay. Learning to walk with it on was extremely challenging. But I was determined to get around just like every other kid who had two normal legs. Every day the doctors and nurses got me up at 6 am, and I practiced walking for an hour. I was sent home after I mastered walking with the prosthesis. That night when I got home, Thomas and I stayed up talking all night.

When I got out of the hospital Mrs. Butler worked hard to get me to start school. I commenced school at age Six and a Half at Mason Springs Elementary. I was bigger than the other kids, but I never felt ashamed or uncomfortable. I was very happy to be in school. The other kids would stare at me, but they were nice and friendly. I remember always humming the songs I would hear my mother sing in class and the teacher would ask, "Who is making that sound?" The other kids would point me out and the teacher would say, "Francis, you are the biggest and oldest, so you should be quiet and be an example to the other kids." I was not trying to disturb her class, singing my mama's songs was all I knew.

I loved going to school and being able to play with the other children, this was a big part of what made school awesome for me. I also did well in school

REV. DR. FRANCIS J. FORD

and made the Honor Roll for most quarters. My favorite subject was Arithmetic. One thing I didn't really like about school was lunch; most times it was bean soup.

I was a very muscular and strong boy so the teacher would always send me and another student named Bobo to pump the water for our class. I loved this task because I enjoyed being useful. I especially, disliked people putting limitations on my ability to accomplish tasks; for example, I was told I could not help set up the Mayflower Pole or carry books, because they thought I would fall. When I got to high school, I was frustrated that the patrols enforced the rule that I had to walk in line with everyone else as this made it difficult for me to keep my balance and keep up with others. The principal took the matter into consideration and as such made a declaration allowing me to walk down the middle of the aisle instead.

Regardless of my disability I had fun growing up. I participated in activities like other kids. I played all positions in baseball. My favorite spot was catching behind home plate. I played football, jumped rope, hopscotch, and marbles, played in the woods and climbed trees. I also found a good bicycle frame which I used to make a bicycle for myself. I rode it with one leg by using strings to tie the fully developed foot to the pedal. I fell many times, but I placed my crutch under my right arm to balance the bike so I could untie my foot from the pedal.

We travelled weekly with Mr. Robert Brown to and from Sunday school. Mrs. Doris Barbara picked us up for choir rehearsal, and I sang in the choir. I loved going to church and eventually became a Sunday School Teacher. I was loved by the church members, and they referred to me as," The Preacher".

I remember my mother telling me at the age of Twelve (12) years old that my full name was in fact

12

Francis Joseph James Paul Ford. It was then that she also prophesied in my life that I was going to become a Preacher.

The weekends at home were miserable and scary because my dad would be fighting and cursing at my mom, but in church I never had to fear that; so I felt free on Sundays as I would be able to go to church and be away from the fighting or cursing. This was the second reason why I loved getting out of the house and going to church. The first was the love for the things of God, and the Word of God; that is where I have always found peace.

CHAPTER 2
MY FATHER

My father was Thirteen (13) years older than my mother. He worked on a farm, earning Six Dollars ($6) per week. He left that job to work at a place called The Spoon Factory (later renamed, Moscow Product) in Pomonkey, Maryland. My father's quiet temperament far exceeded my mom's, except when he drank alcoholic beverages.

Pay day was on Fridays, and this was synonymous with his alcohol consumption. Although he was not a very heavy drinker, the little he would consume was enough to intoxicate him. Whenever he drank alcohol, he would conceal the bottle in his pocket. Regardless, at times I would see him drinking it and felt afraid. The alcohol brought out a frightening reality that was pronounced on his face. Soon after drinking, he would fight and curse my mom. Growing up I have no memory of him

14

fussing with anyone else except mom. She would never fight him back. At one time, I witnessed him treating her as though she was a punching bag. She was the recipient of punches and slaps, yet surprisingly she did not retaliate. She remained a submissive wife, and a nurturing, loving mother. This was the unwritten law of their relationship – despite any abuse, the wife must remain submitted. He was never deprived of his dinner, cleaned and ironed clothes or a clean home. Once, she called the police and he was locked up but received bail and was back home the following day at 2 am. I could not sleep during the weekends. I remembered, many times my siblings just witnessed the abuse and cried.

Despite his behavior towards our mother, we never disrespected him. I felt severe resentment and hatred for him to the point that I thought about killing him several times for always abusing my mother. This was another unwritten law – children must never disrespect the elderly, especially parents. The community raised every child and could also discipline a rude child. As a child you were not permitted to rebut an adult. Their words were final.

The only positive thing I can recall him telling me, was "boy if you want anything you got to work for it, and anything that does not long (belong) to you don't touch it." Dad was a hard worker who thought it wrong to not work. He worked until it was time to go to bed. His quiet demeanour was evident throughout the week until payday – the dreaded day. Dad believed that, after you had worked hard all week, you owe yourself a bit of pampering. His method was drinking. On his way home after work on Fridays he and his younger brother Leo, and a friend named Bill, made it their routine to stop at the liquor store. They purchased and drank alcohol on Friday nights and continued drinking until late Sunday evening. Then he went to bed to be sober for work on Monday. Dad also smoked but not consistently; a pack of cigarettes lasted about Three (3) months.

My father did his own farming on the property our home was on. He reared tobacco, corn, sweet/white potatoes and herbs. The farm produced the best greens in town, kale, collard green and string beans. We had to go into the field to cut and strip tobacco. Tobacco was the money crop, and this was the way we bought toys for Christmas. Swan's General store bought a lot of our kale and resold it to the community. Tobacco was harvested in September. The process included cutting and sparing (putting the tobacco on a stick) then hanging them in the barns for curing. After curing (allowing the tobacco to change from green to brown), the next stage was stripping. This separates the second, bright, dark and tips from each other, each was bundled differently. One stalk produced four different components: the second, bright, dark and the tips. The second is the first part but was not of the highest quality. It had holes in it, probably because it was close to the earth. The bright was the big money component, these are the big pretty leaves without holes. The dark was the third component which were leaves that had a dark color. These yielded good money as well. Then the tips which are the last part of the tobacco. It did not earn a lot of money but was a good sell. If we got up feeling sick, father would say eat a bowl of oatmeal and go and work it off. Our life was rough and hard, but we made it by God's grace.

Chicken and hogs that we reared were killed during November as we got ready for Thanksgiving. Since there were no refrigerators, the meats were cured to preserve them. The meat was cured in a shed we called the meat house; the process involved packing the meats with salt and red pepper and then tying these packages to the ceiling. The meat stayed there until we were ready to consume it, this meat lasted for as long as Four (4) months.

My dad, although raised as a Catholic, never went to church except for funerals. He cemented in my belief system the following words: "Boy, if you want anything you will have to work hard for it." My Mother was able to read as she would read her catalogues and mails; she had at least a Third grade level education. My father on the other hand was illiterate. I came to this realization one day when we went to the hospital and the doctor asked him to spell Pisgah and he couldn't. I told my mom when I got home, and she informed me of his status. As a boy, he was not allowed to go to school because he had to stay home and take care of his mother, sisters and brothers. Despite his educational limitations, he insisted on us doing our homework and learning to read and write.

He was very skilled with his hands. He could not afford to buy wagons nor wheel barrows, so he made his own.

Eventually, dad acquired his own car, a Model T, and it was his pride achievement. The battery of the car was located under the driver's seat. Occasionally, as he drove to and from home, the car would hit a bump (we called them mud holes) and the battery would fall out and we had to get out the car to go look for it and put it back in place, even in the dark. The roads were not asphalt or gravel, they were all dirt. Dad later bought a 1939 Two-seater Chevrolet. We used wooden benches as the rear seats. Sometimes those benches turned over, especially when he went around corners. He also acquired a 1949 Green Ford. This easily seated six persons – three at the front and three at the back. His last car was a 1951 station wagon Green Chrysler.

In the summer we went fishing, a lot, in preparation for the winter. We caught numerous herrings from Mason Spring River/Lake, which we salted down. They were stored in a Fifty-Five gallon wooden drum. We were blessed, and in a position to help others. Mother helped her siblings out with food. Once there was an argument between dad and mom. He complained saying, "People were coming to the house dragging my food away." I think he was talking about her helping her family. My mother's kind heart propelled her to ignore some verbal accusations from my dad. My mother had two brothers, Uncle Bus and Uncle Charlie, who did not not come to the house when dad was there, because they resented him.

My father was just crazy, he sometimes walked up and down in the yard saying, "I see car tracks, who was here?" He was not one for much company. However, he loved playing the guitar, especially listening to or playing HillBilly Music. Uncle Leo played the violin, and they made a great team while someone sang. Dad gave me a guitar, and in high school I learned to play the trumpet and then the French horn. Mom was born in 1925 and died in 1957 and dad was born in 1912 and died in 1996, I believe from colon cancer.

CHAPTER 3
DEATH

One Sunday night, mom, dad, Thomas, and I were at Lucky Strikes; a dance hall, operated by my father's sister, Aunt Nelly. Occasionally, about four or five times per year, the trip to visit my aunt was done. Father was not interested in dance, so he and I stayed in the car outside looking through the window at times. Thomas and mom went inside. Dad and his sister had a good relationship.

Father decided he was going home early after a while. Mom told him to go ahead, she would see him when she got home. I stayed back with mom and Thomas. On the way home, mom stopped by her sister's house (Aunt Sadie), we stayed there for a while. I remember her, laying on the floor that summer night. Thinking back now, she has never been out of the house this long, makes me wonder if she somehow knew that something was going to go wrong.

After a while we left Aunt Sadie's home and walked the ten-minute journey home. Mom knocked on the door while I was standing at her right side. Dressed in a pair of slacks and a polo t-shirt, my dad opened the door rapidly as if he had snatched it. Although it was dark I could see inside from the only light in the house, the little kerosene oil lamps. My eyes were suddenly captured not by him standing at the door opening, but by the shotgun in his hand. This was a single barrel shotgun that he used for hunting rabbits and squirrels. All my siblings were standing inside the house behind him. His face was pleasant, and everything seemed alright. Then it happened. It was so fast. He said nothing; she said nothing. But that silence was interrupted by a sound that changed our lives forever. My father shot my mother in the chest with a 12 gauge shotgun.

24

I felt the heat, and powder from the bullet shell on my face, then the weight of the gun as it collided with my head. This happened because I jumped up and grabbed him. My head was busted open and I fell to the ground. With blood gushing down my face from my head, I still managed to grab him by the leg. He slipped out of his shoe and took off running down across the field in front of the house. I could not chase him because I cannot run. Thomas, who stayed back to enjoy the dance a bit longer, got home at this time. I was fourteen and Thomas was Sixteen years old.

She was gone! My mother laid lifeless wearing her floral dress, in a pool of her own blood. Why did he kill my kind, soft spoken angelic singing voice mother? He took from us our most treasured gift from God. Many questions poured in my mind from the anger I felt towards my father. He abused her and she took it without retaliation and now she is dead. Abuse must never be tolerated. An Excerpt from Domestic Shelters. Org says:

> *Alarming statistics indicate that, as you read this short sentence, a woman has become the victim of assault. According to the Partnership Against Domestic Violence, every 9 seconds, another woman in the U.S. is beaten.* Every nine seconds. It's a sobering reality for one in four women in the U.S. will experience domestic violence in their lifetime, most frequently by someone they know. Female victims most commonly first experience domestic violence between the ages of 18-24 (38.6%), followed by age 11-17 (22.4%), age 35-44 (6.8%) and age 45+ (2.5%). Almost one out of five or 16.3% of murder victims in the U.S. were killed by an intimate partner; women account for two out of three murder victims killed by an intimate partner.

Jimmy ran off to tell Aunt Sadie, and the neighbors telephoned the Police Department. Meanwhile, Thomas and I looked for dad to kill him. He was never located, until the police came, searched and found him. He jumped in and hid himself in a nearby well at his mother's place. That night was long and sad. I remember it vividly. An ambulance arrived and took him and I to the hospital. I received Six (6) sutures (stitches) to the right side of my head, then was released from the hospital. A relative took me home from the hospital. He stayed at the hospital for four days and was treated for hyperthermia. After which he was taken to jail. My siblings clung together and cried uncontrollably. I cried but never allowed my siblings to know. It was not pride but rather being strong for them. Our poor family was shattered – no mother, no father, only trusting God.

A week or so later we were all divided up like sheep, among my parent's siblings, by the Department of Social Service. Aunt Nellie Bowman had in her care Roman, Howard, Spaulding, Albert and Curtis. Curtis was about Nine and a Half months old. Aunt Martha Keys had in her care Bertha and Minnie (Peaches, deceased). Aunt

Margaret Grayer had in her care Gloria, Maggie, and Evelyn. Aunt Rene Gray had Charles in her care. Aunt Viola Ford took me in her care. Thomas was on his own. I do not remember him being told that he was placed under a specific family member's care. He stayed mainly with Aunt Shirley Brown. After a while Thomas was driving and would come visit me and the other siblings. I would get to see my siblings every week except Maggie, Evelyn, and Gloria, who lived far away. So, we would only see them occasionally.

My dad went on trial and had a white attorney representing him. Thomas and I went occasionally to the courthouse during the proceedings. Jimmy, who was thirteen, went once. Dad was sentenced to Twelve years in prison but served Three and a Half years on good behavior, with orders to stay out of trouble. During his time of incarceration, I visited him Three times with Aunt Nellie, before we saw him, we were taken to a room and searched. Then

28

he came out from his cell clad in a full orange uniform. We spoke through iron bars with a guard observing everything we did. The first time I saw him in prison was difficult. However, I eventually got used to it. My brother Clarence said dad once told him that he thought another man was in the yard and he was the one that he shot at. Dad and I never had any conversation about what happened. Upon his release from prison, he went to live with his sister Aunt Anna. He went back to work at his old job at the spoon factory and stayed there until it closed down. At the factory there was a tank with constant boiling water which was used in the spoon making process. One day dad accidentally fell in and was severely burnt all over. He was rushed to the hospital and remained in the intensive unit for approximately Four months. When we visited him, we had to be dressed in gowns, face masks and hoods.

After the factory closed, he did odd jobs cleaning the yard of a liquor store. He also did landscaping which he loved. He did this until he got sick, went to the hospital, and died on October 5th, 1996. He was diagnosed with colon cancer. He fought it for a little over a year until he lost the fight.

CHAPTER 4
LIFE AFTER MOM

We no longer had mom to play hopscotch, baseball and talk to us about life. Mom made baseballs from old socks. She pooled them together and sewed the ends. I grew up very upset with God, wondering, "Why?" Since He knows all things, why did He let this happen? This tormented me for many years. Sometime later, Aunt Viola's sister, her husband and son George came to live with us. George was two years older than I was. I was elated when he came to live with us because there were mostly girls in the house and two boys, who were much younger than I was. I was the only one in the house who went to church; I still remained actively involved in church throughout this time regardless.

George worked at a Pool Room. I talked to him about church, and he talked mostly about Pool. George was always at my side. We had a lifetime close bond. After some time, George was converted to Christianity and became a great servant for The Lord. He led praise and worship service, until he was taken home to be with The Lord in 2017, when he died a natural death. He and his wife, Faye, always came to visit Mount Hope Missionary Baptist Church where I preached every year on Mother's Day. If I never saw him any other time of the year, I knew I would see him on this day. I did visit him occasionally when time permitted. His wife would cook and bake bread as though it was a feast. Faye was a cooking woman. She loved cooking and whatever she made was A, B, C Delicious.

As a teenager, I had a job every weekend working for Mrs. Compton, a white neighbor. For a long time, I raked her yard, clipped her flowers, cut, and trimmed her grass. She lived less than a mile from Aunt Viola's house where I was still living. I would walk there every Saturday morning. She did not let me inside her house for about six months but allowed me to always be on the back porch. She would lay money around on the porch where the flowers were, then she would ask me if I had seen it. She started out with small amounts first, then the sum got larger. She would put down money and say, "I don't remember where I put it". I assumed she was tempting me to see if I could be trusted. After realizing I did not steal, she relaxed her fears and I was allowed to go not only in the house but there were times she sent me in her bedroom to bring her things off her dresser like pencils, envelopes etc. And yes, money was also visible laying around – she and her husband were both elderly.

Living with my aunt, I continued going to school and worked at a local restaurant at nights washing dishes. Some days I slept all day, no one woke me for school. So when I woke, it was time to go to work again. I felt terrible; like I was losing it. I had to hitchhike a ride to get to work, which was not too bad but getting back home at night was a challenge. Some nights, I would have to walk home; sometimes by the time I got home it was time to go to school. There was another guy who did the journey with me. That helped to not let the walk be lonely. My feet hurt. The distance from work to home was about Twenty Two miles. No public transportation, bus or train operated in Maryland at that time. Washington DC was the only place bus services were offered at the time.

After a while I became interested in shooting pool. Sunday was the day they played Pool; I began playing and as a result started missing out on church. I became comfortable and just never went back to church. At this time I was 18 years old ;I became a backslider, out in the world and I quit school also. At first, I felt guilty but then after a while I felt like nothing was wrong. The writer of 1

REV. DR. FRANCIS J. FORD

Timothy addressed the issue of sinning and no longer feeling guilty (Chapter 4:1-2):

> "Now the Spirit speaketh expressly, that in the latter times some shall depart from the faith, giving heed to seducing spirits, and doctrines of devils; Speaking lies in hypocrisy; having their conscience seared with a hot iron…"

Still being ambitious, I got a construction job finishing concrete in basement floors. Over the previous years my prosthesis never got the required maintenance and was in need of desperate repairs. The belt that held it around my waist was broken, so I figured out another way to keep it on. This I did by locking the knee by bending it. Everything was fine until one day the boss and foreman were watching me work. I got so caught up with them watching and saying how good the work looked, I forgot about my leg, and went to move over some more to smooth the concrete out without precaution and the prosthesis got stuck in the concrete and came off right before their eyes. The next day I was dismissed because it was against the law in those days for the handicapped/disabled to be employed in construction.

I cried all the way to the East Over Shopping Center at the Howard Johnson restaurant, where there was a sign, which read, 'help wanted'. I went in and applied and was hired on the spot. I worked as a dishwasher there for a year. This job was close to Washington DC, so I moved in with my Aunt Margaret Riley who lived in that state. The convenience of living in close proximity to work was welcomed, but the negativity from my Aunt was unbearable. She always criticized me and would say degrading things like I would never become anything, and that I would not be successful in life. Regardless of her unpleasant connotations, I decided to capitalize on her negative words and demeaning attitude. I used them to encourage myself and became more eager and determined to prove her wrong by succeeding.

Driven by my ambitious nature and love for nice clothing, I always had a job. At the age of Twenty years old, my Social Service counselor helped me to get registered in a trade school, where I took up shoe repair, fixing electric appliances including television and radios, upholstery and plumbing. I made Seven (7) cents an hour fixing appliances. Whenever customers bought the items, I would be given a small percentage. Working all week from 8 am to 4 pm, my check would at times be $2.75 for the week. I stayed in that job for 2 years.

My ambition was to do mechanics, but I was never accepted because of my disability. So again I started working in restaurants washing dishes and being a short order cook. As a short order cook I made simple quick meals that did not require any expertise. I later worked at a car wash at East Over and at Canada Dry Soda Company. I loaded trucks using a forklift. I was later removed from loading trucks to just fuel the trucks and check their oil.

I then ventured into learning the city with the intent of operating a taxi. One day while studying for my driver's license, aunt Margaret noticed what I was doing and said, "You are too dumb, you can never learn to drive here in Washington DC." I proved her wrong through the help of God. I made it; I got my license and became a Cab Driver in DC where I made good money. Aunty never asked me for money as the childcare services gave her a check for my room and board every month.

When I met my first wife Diane, she had a boyfriend at the time who took her to my aunt's house occasionally and left her there. One day she said she wanted to go to the store, and I walked her there. On our way back from the store, I heard a voice behind me say this is going to be your wife. I turned around and there was no one. After that day, I did not see Diane for about five years. I thought about her occasionally, but as a young man having fun I dated other women. One night while operating the taxi cab, a light skinned lady with long pretty hair flagged down my cab; I pulled over and it was Diane, I picked her up and we talked all the way to her destination and she gave me her number. She told me her boyfriend was in jail, he had refused to work honestly and made stealing his routine. We dated for a while, and then Rev. John Ford (not a relative) did marital counselling with us for over a year. The counselling was done once per week. It included a lot of reading and answering of questions. We got married at the local church at the end of the year's counselling. Our wedding theme was royal blue and white. She looked stunningly beautiful, as always. She was 5'2" and weighed about 170 lbs. Diane was easy to get along with; always very friendly and compassionate. She was raised by her aunt because her mother was deceased, and her father was not a part of her life.

However, when I eventually met her father, he said to me, "you better take care of my daughter". At our wedding, we were both supported by a lot of her relatives. They were very happy for her. We moved into an apartment complex in Washington DC and there we began our life together.

Diane was at first a housewife. Later she worked at a drugstore; she packed the shelves and attended to customers. Diane was in church, but I was not at that time. She sang in the choir, ushered, and taught the very young children. I later began revisiting church with Diane.

We never had biological kids. Diane and I loved and wanted children of our own. We tried getting pregnant for Three (3) years and had one miscarriage. Subsequently, we decided to take the adoption route. We adopted Seven (7) children, namely: Angela, Kontina, Shakida, Devon, Walter, Sierra and Gregory. Walter and Sierra are biological siblings. Walter is very adventurous. I am proud of all my children, but I am super proud of Walter. He completed college with a major in writing and has already written a book. He lives in North Carolina and loves rock climbing.

Sierra is the challenging one of the bunch. She reported us to the authorities. We were investigated, but they found no truth or evidence to substantiate her claims. She kept floating between foster homes. She is still troubled, and I will continue believing in God for her miracle.

Out of all the children, Angela was the 'talker'. Her teacher complained about her constant talking in class. She is hardworking and loves cars like me. Although she went to school and majored in computers, she spent all her adult life selling cars.

Shakida, now deceased, was very adventurous, funny, mischievous, and mouthy. She was strong willed and did what she wanted to do. She wanted to live fast. She stole our car twice while we were sleeping. One night she hit a preacher's parked car. It was reported to the police as a hit and run. Shakida was interviewed for about Thirty minutes before she confessed that it was her. She fell in love, but never got married. When she became an adult, she went and found her biological family back in DC. She leaves behind two children, who are with her biological family and friends.

Kontina is very loving, caring and very compassionate. Like me, she loves and fears the Lord. She also looks a lot like me. She was a smart, good child. However, she decided to stop going to school. Thus, we sent her to a camp which was designed to bring troubled children in alignment with good practices. She met a young man at the camp and decided to get married. I was too upset to marry them, but my pastor did it. She is married and has two beautiful children, Jesse Jr., who is very respectful and pleasant, and Jayah, who is normally well mannered but can be mouthy at

42

times. We have a close bond, and keep in touch at all times. She has major health issues and tries to keep the family together.

Devon never got married but had two children with his girlfriend.

Angela was the first we adopted, and she was also the eldest. All seven were between six and nine months when we got custody of them; they were all from the Foster Care Services. Diane and I decided to tell them that they were adopted. We also told them the reasons why they were originally in Foster Care. This became a blessing, as neighbours told them that they were adopted. The children lived well with each other, they had their moments of disagreement but those were settled peacefully. I was happy to have my own wife and children. I love big families and was overjoyed to have my own. Finally, I had children to look up to for guidance and protection.

Gregory was a baby when we adopted him. We later found out that he had multiple sclerosis. Medical providers and friends would encourage us to take him back to the system. One doctor told us that he would never live to see the age of twelve; he is now Forty Five years old. He is dependent on someone for necessary daily activities as he is unable to feed himself, speak, or walk, but he is very smart in finding ways to communicate with his eyes, hands, and sounds. We took Gregory to the doctor for examination when he was Nine months old and received huge assistance from the John Hopkins Hospital in Baltimore. We had a motor chair that he used to move around. Gregory said he wanted to be baptized and we did so in a bathtub. He lives in Baltimore now and has a Facebook page. We Facetime so we can see him. Angela acted as though she adopted him. He loves Michael Jordan and she ensured that he got everything from Michael Jordan merchandise.

Whatever Gregory wants, it is not too expensive; Angie is going to make it happen. She cares for him even to this day. After Diane died, it was too much for me to care for him alone. I was forced to place him at an assisted living facility.

CHAPTER 5
THE CALL

One evening I got off from work, while on my way home on Dean Ave in Washington DC, I suddenly got very hungry. I called on the Lord and asked what was happening to me. I heard a voice say, "When you get home, tell your wife you will start going to church next Sunday." When I got home, the table was all set, my dinner was ready. I sat down to eat, and I suddenly became full as though I had already eaten; I could not eat a bite. Diane asked, "What is wrong with you?" I told her, "The Lord told me to tell you that on Sunday I will start going to church." She looked at me and replied, "I do not believe you." That night I did not eat but rather got my bible and laid across the bed and read John 14:1-6 repeatedly. I did not sleep. Yet the following morning, I felt as though I had gotten a good rest, I went to work and drove my truck all day with the scripture playing over and over in my mind.

I resumed attending church and found my way back to God. My family and I joined Woodland Village Baptist church, where Rev. Yancy Warren was the pastor. I thought I could run and do my own thing, so I started a gospel group in 1975, called The Gospel Soul Seekers. We celebrated our first anniversary on June 6, 1976. We are still singing, but only three of the original members are alive – Francis I Ford, Philip Hill, and myself Francis J. Ford.

I assisted with the choir, led prayer service, and after being there for about a year or more Rev. Warren appointed me as a Deacon. I attended training and went to different classes before I officially became a Deacon. After that I was ordained and installed as Chairman Deacon. While serving as a Deacon I realized that God had another calling for me. The Spirit of The Lord kept telling me to inform my Pastor that God called me to preach. I ignored the call for a while and was tormented. The word came almost every day at midday. I had sleepless nights. Eventually I went to the doctor to find out what was wrong. The doctor said I was eating too late.

Yet, I still heard God calling. I had nowhere to run or hide, so finally I told my pastor what God said. About Seven (7) months later, Rev. Warren set a date for me to Minister to the congregation; the date was January 12th, 1981, at 3:30 pm. That Sunday I did my trial sermon entitled, "I found the answer" which was taken from John 14:1-6. Afterwards I was approved and licensed by the church to preach the Gospel of Jesus Christ. I enrolled at The Washington Baptist Theological Seminary that same year in October and attended classes five nights per week. Sessions were 5pm - 8pm, Mondays to Fridays. At the end of four years, I graduated in June 1985 and was ordained in 1986.

Rev. Dr. John Franklin conducted the training for ordination, but the ordination service was done by Rev. Dr. Andrew Fowler. At that time, I understood why God prevented Thomas and I from finding our dad the night he murdered our mother. God blocked me from being incarcerated; prison was not God's will for my life, but preaching His Word was.

In 1989, I retired from my job as a truck driver after exactly Twenty (20) years, Two (2) months and Two (2) days. The last Ten (10) years prior to retirement were accident free. I applied and was accepted at the Washington Theological Seminary where I achieved a Diploma in Ministry. During my study, I wanted to quit in the fourth and final year as it became financially challenging, but Diane said no. She was adamant that I stay in school, so she sought employment to support me through the final year of that program. She found a job as a laundry attendant. I then enrolled in Virginia Theological

49

Seminary in 1992 and in 1997 I completed a Bachelor's and Master's in Theology. During my studies at Virginia Theological Seminary, I enrolled at Strayer College in 1996 to get my High School Diploma which I received in the year 2000. All my studies were done from home. While studying, I had some challenges with trigonometry but overall I did well.

I went to Mount Hope to play in a Male Chorus for a period of time after which I joined the church there. I was asked by the Pastor to be his assistant and the church voted, and it was cemented. After a while, Rev. Jesse Williams was unable to function as the Lead Pastor and I became the Interim Pastor. The church wanted me to be Interim for another Six months, but one lady pointed out that I had held the interim position long enough, so why not make me the Pastor. They all agreed, and I was installed as the Lead Pastor in 2001. Dianne contracted the Flu, so she went to the doctor. After getting a flu shot, she got worse. The doctor said the Flu would do its course, but she never recovered. Diane died in November of 2005. This was a difficult period for me. It was not easy losing my wife of Thirty Seven (37) years. Like when my mother died, I had to be strong again. This time it was for the children, especially Gregory. The church gave me welcomed time off to grieve. I wanted to officiate her funeral and began preparing my notes but realized I would not be able to. My assistant, Rev. White, officiated the service.

I continued pastoring and enrolled in Wilbur Waters School of Religion. I did additional courses in sermon preparations and pursued my Doctorate in Theology. I taught Homiletics there for a year. While writing my doctoral thesis I had a stroke which caused me to pause my studies. I was a member of Mount Hope for Twenty One (21) years and pastored there for Seventeen (17) years. I resigned on the 31st of November 2018. My resignation became necessary as I was unable to stand for long periods. I thought it best to make way for the next leader who would be able to carry on the mission of the church. At my resignation service, the President of the school awarded me with my Doctorate Certificate.

Lord, I thank you for all the churches that supported me in the ministry as I pressed on in service. My greatest supporters can be found in Mount Hope Missionary Baptist church, located in Nanjemoy Maryland, where I was honored to be the Pastor for over Seventeen (17) years. I am so glad they embraced me, took me into their family and we were able to get things done. Mount Hope, a church where we became one big family. I am grateful for the Deacons and Deaconesses of the church as well as those who served as Church Clerks, wonderful Trustees and Youth/Sunday School Leaders. As a church we honor these people: Minister Wallace, Sis. Tracey Locus,

Deaconess Beverly Swan, and Sis. Leslie Gibson. It would be remiss of me not to mention how grateful I am for Deaconess Diane Heard, though she has gone to be with The Lord. Our church stayed together thanks to the leadership of The Holy Spirit; God always made a way. Yes, I miss Mount Hope. I prayed about my leaving, and I knew it was time to go. Thankfully, I had good associates to leave in charge of the church, Rev. Martin Greenwood, Min. Rita Wallace, Min. Kevin Thomas and Rev.Dr. Ruby Thomas.

All my thanks goes to God for how He brought me through the many storms of life. I have immense appreciation for Mount Hope, Smith Chapel United Methodist Church, Oak Grove Baptist Church, Macedonia Baptist Church, Alexandria Chapel Methodist Church, Woodland Village Baptist Church, Sylvan Vista Baptist Church and Holy Sanctuary.

It is due to point out that the Pastor of the Holy Sanctuary Church, Bishop Timothy Warren is the son of my initial Pastor Yancy Warren. I had the pleasure of watching and helping to nurture Timothy throughout his young years and is blessed to see himself actualize and blossom into a true Man of God. Timothy gave me the honor of doing my first commencement speech in 2020 at their annual graduation ceremony; utilizing my Doctorate for the first time. To God be the Glory as He has made the way possible for me to use each accreditation that I acquired regardless of my limitations/disability.

CHAPTER 6
LOVE AGAIN

On a Wednesday night after a prayer meeting at Mount Hope missionary Baptist church, Diane and I stopped at IHOP (International House of Pancakes) in Clinton Maryland Prince George's County to eat. Our server was a young lady named Elmarie. I did not know her at that time, it was my first time seeing her, she was wearing her uniform: white shirt, black pants, and blue apron. She greeted my wife and I with a very pleasant smile which showcased her pretty white teeth. As she spoke her accent was distinctly not American. She was dark skinned, petite in figure, very beautiful with short curly blond hair. Even though it was the first time seeing her, something strange happened to me. I cannot adequately explain it. It seemed like a voice was saying, "she is the one for you." I knew the same voice had told me Diane was the one before I married her. I protested, "God what is this? I do not cheat; I love my wife. I have never looked at another woman or even had a desire for anyone but my wife." I love God and honor his word. I am a father, and an example for my sons. I could not understand why I had this feeling for this server who I was meeting for the first time. Time passed and I forgot about that night, and I never went back to that IHOP.

Two months later Diane died on November 5th, 2005. My whole world was shaken. I felt lost. I cried, but I tried to stay strong for the children. In late January I went back to IHOP, and I sat in Angela's service section, an African lady, so as to avoid Elmarie. However, another day I went to IHOP for breakfast and the manager sat me in a section. I soon realized the same young lady I saw a couple months ago that I had the strange feeling about was the server. She was fair to the eyes, and I realized I still had that feeling. I looked at her hands, she was not wearing a wedding band, so I assumed she was not married and was available. I began frequenting IHOP daily, and I quickly identified that she remembered my order for breakfast, lunch, and dinner. She knew how I liked my steak and my eggs and if it were lunch, she knew the options I preferred so she would simply ask, "a salad or a sandwich?"

One day I asked her what she did after work and on her days off. Her response was, "I stay home and talk to my family back in Jamaica." I followed up by asking her about her hobbies, and she told me she likes bowling. She went bowling in Maine, and she was pretty good at it. This was good news to my ears because I bowled in a bowling league. I asked her out to bowl the next time she was off, which she let me know was the following Tuesday. She would not give me her number, so I gave her mine. I told her to call me so we could go out and eat and then go bowling. She agreed to go, so we decided on a time, noon that Tuesday.

I woke up that Tuesday morning happy, excited, and overwhelmed with joy. But it was now noon, and she had not called. So, I am thinking, 'Ok, maybe she will call soon.' Looking at my watch and my phone, it is now 12:15 pm; still no call. The devil said you have been stood up. By 12:30 pm, still no call. By now I am getting frustrated. So, I said to myself, if she doesn't call by 1 pm, I'm going without her. At 12:45 pm, still no call. So, I decided I was going to leave. My cell phone was still in my hand, so as to make sure I would not miss the call. At 1 pm I reached for the door and the phone rang. It was her voice.

She gave me her address and I happily drove to pick her up in my blue 2005 suburban. I pulled up, she came out wearing a pair of blue jeans and a brown plaid shirt, looking beautiful as always. We went out bowling, had a good time, I then took her to my favorite place to eat Golden Coral. She was only used to eating her culture's food, so choosing was a bit challenging but I helped by explaining and making suggestions. After dinner I brought her home, she said she had a good time. I went home feeling good because to me this was progress.

After that I continued going to IHOP and sitting in her section. We became more acquainted, and she told me she had no ride to work at the time. I delivered newspapers for the Washington Post at the time. I told her I'm up early in the mornings so I could take her to and from work. The road that she walked on to get to the county bus stop had a troubled house where guys on drugs hung out.

When I pick her up from work in the evening, I would make sure that if she needed to go grocery shopping, I would take her. I would call when I got home to ask if she had dinner and what she ate. I realized now that her routine was to go home and be by herself, so I would ask her to ride with me in the evenings. I would take her with me if I had errands to run and took the opportunity to show her the country areas where I grew up. We started going out for dinner most evenings; we realized we both love steak and seafood.

When we drove around, we would talk about the Bible. She was very knowledgeable about the word of God. We are compatible in that we were raised the same way, love to travel, and accepted the same things culturally. Also, from playing music while riding along I realized she had a beautiful voice. One evening I asked her to sing me a song. I was in awe; she started singing amazing grace. I have always wished that I had a wife that could sing, but Diane never liked singing. I'm now Sixty (60) years of age and God has blessed me with a wife that loves to sing. I feel happy and alive again. We sang together as we drove along, having our own praise party, just glorifying God. I was mentally, physically, and spiritually renewed.

One night my son Devon asked me to give him a ride to his friend's house. I asked Elmarie if she would accompany me; she did. On our way back while we were alone, I said these words to her, "Would you be willing to spend the next Thirty-Six years of my life with me?" I then told her that she didn't have to answer right away but pray and fast about it. She asked, "Why Thirty- Six?" I answered, "I'm now Sixty, and I have asked God to let me live to see the age of Ninety-Six, so because I asked God, I believe I have Thirty-Six more years to go."

A month went by and she said nothing of the matter. So, one evening as we went for dinner I asked her, "Did you give any thoughts to my question? Have you been praying about it?" I think it was then she realized that I was not joking; we usually laughed and joked a lot. She then told me that she would ask her mom to help her pray about it. A week later, she told me that she got the answer from a dream that her mother had. In the vision there were three fish of different sizes and God said to her that the smallest of the three was the choiced one. At that time two other individuals who were financially set were expressing an interest in her. Also I was the only one of the three who had a disability/ limitation. Elmarie at that present moment knew that I was the one to choose as of the three I was the least financially set; She chose to obey God regardless of the fact that she realized that the road ahead would be a challenge.

I spoke with her mother; we had a long good, pleasant talk and our spirit connected right away. I knew she was a child of God, one who truly loves God. We prayed after the conversation. Elmarie was well trained and working for The Lord; her mother taught her well. After we got to know each other better, she helped me deliver newspapers on days that she was off work. We spent a lot of time together while dating. We would sit in the car late after midnight talking and singing. She taught me songs from her culture, and I taught her songs I loved and sang with the Soul Seekers. One of our favorite songs is by Eddie Ruth Bradford, "Jesus, you held on, even when I let go."

I could see that she was quite comfortable with me, evidenced by her putting up her feet on the dashboard, as we drove along. Elmarie trusted me. She started divulging sensitive personal information; she told me about her two sons, deceased husband, and immigration status. After making me aware of these things, she questioned me, "Do you still want to marry me?" My reply was a confident, "Yes!" She pressed, "Are you sure?" My answer remained unchanged. I said yes.

Elmarie talked to her family every day and in those times, we had to go to the gas station to purchase phone cards. It was through phone calls that I became acquainted with her two sons, Oshae, Seven and Miguel, Twelve. Elmarie introduced me to them as her fiancé and before we were married, they were happy to call me Dad. They were wonderful boys and grew up to be pleasant and respectful young men. They both came to the USA at the age of Eight and Thirteen and attended school here. Miguel, a Towson Graduate with a Bachelor's in Accounting, works at Cohen, one of the top accounting firms in the US as a Senior Accountant. Oshae, still in College presently, pursuing a Degree in Financing. Even more commendable, they both love the Lord. They grew up in church and used their wonderful voices as members of the choir.

I went on a trip to Florida with a friend, Francis Burns, and some of the children; this was during my vacation the July of the year before I married Elmarie. I wished that I could take her with me. It was my hope to buy her a wedding ring during the trip. Not wanting to guess her ring size, I asked her about it, but she was also clueless as to the matter. So, I told her to go get her finger sized. The trip was cut short due to an incident that happened to Elmarie. I called her one evening and she was not her usual self. I knew something was wrong; there was no laughter in her tone. After enquiring about what was wrong, she informed me someone had broken into her room and robbed her. The thief took all the money that she had at home: her salary, the tips, partner draw and even spare coins. She had all this money at home because she had not gotten time to go to the bank. This nerve-wracking experience left her too scared to sleep in the room. I started driving back that night.

On my return from Florida, we agreed on a wedding date. I told her I was a 'preacher man' and could not date her for long. We both agreed that based on 2 Corinthians 6:3, *"Giving no offence in anything, that the ministry be not blamed,"* it may invite onlookers to have a misgiving as to the nature of our relationship. We were excited about getting married. At this time, it was a bit confusing and frustrating because we were ready and longing to be together, but out of custom I needed to wait a year before remarrying after the loss of my spouse. This was a custom that I picked up from my mother. I explained this to her, and we agreed to wait until December the 9th 2006 to get married. Elmarie and I were joined together in Holy matrimony on 12/ 09/2006 at Mount Hope Missionary Baptist church By Rev. Carl Messiah, Pastor of Pleasant Grove Missionary Baptist Church in Marbury Maryland (now Pastor Emeritus). I have since changed Elmarie's name to 'My Joy'; she makes me extremely happy.

Rev. Messiah is a very close friend. When others realized I was planning to marry Elmarie, our age difference and her immigration status did not go unnoticed. Rumors started circulating that she was marrying me for a green card and that she was way too young for me.

When I needed a friend, I spoke with Rev. Messiah and Rev. Hancock, who would both say, "Ford, if you love that gal, marry her." I was encouraged by this. Kontina, ever my supporter, was also in my corner. I love all my kids, but Kontina and I are so much alike that we have a special bond. She helped me embrace my choice when she told me this, "Dad, you need to get her a ring, let's make it official."

Our wedding theme was royal blue (my favorite color) and silver. All the children except Angie attended. The entire church was invited. Elmarie, not having family in the States at the time, chose Kontina to be her Maid of Honor. She was fond of Kontina and her children because they had always been accepting of her, and she was always comfortable around them. I called Angie after the wedding to find out why she never showed up. I was sure that she would be there; her absence was greatly disappointing. She never gave me a good reason, so I left it as it was. But this hurt me to my heart. I was glad that despite how close Greg and Angie are, he and Elmarie have a very good relationship.

Elmarie and I went to Pocono in Pennsylvania for our one week honeymoon, after the marriage ceremony. We got to Pennsylvania very late that night; it was a long ride. It was wonderful driving; just the two of us. I remember having thoughts of finally seeing her legs; she always wore long pants. The morning after our wedding night we both fasted and stayed in prayer until six pm.

That evening we consummated our marriage, and it was wild, passionate, and unforgettable to say the least. I told My Joy that night that I will always want her to be my girlfriend instead of a wife. She looked surprised and asked why, I replied girlfriends are always fun and exciting, but wives tend to get complacent.

We knew that we would face challenges, spiritually and physically, as we united because I am a leader and she would have to take on a role that she knew was going to be tough. Being Thirty years younger than me, it seemed that most church members would not expect her to live up to their expectations of a First Lady. Fortunately, Elmarie had the mindset that she is called to please only God and be who He made her to be.

It was still a mentally and emotionally exacting ride. The negative message of Angie not attending the wedding was still fresh in our memories. Thank God, Mount Hope embraced their new First Lady. True, a few attitudes were noted occasionally with a few people. But God helped us by giving us people that supported us. To Elmarie He assigned a support group. Most notably Mama Heard, she became like a mother to Elmarie. During those early days she was always calling and checking in on us; she still checks in with us till this day.

Elmarie was not the typical First Lady that a Baptist church sees. For one, she was much younger. Also, unlike other First ladies, she never liked wearing hats; she tried it a few times, but it was just not her thing. Moreover, there were cultural differences: she would stand, clap, and shout; she was quick to pray, which was not seen often in the Baptist church. Overall, I believe the congregation looked up to her with respect as my wife. She was very outspoken and demonstrated stern leadership qualities. However, she never wanted to be a Deaconess. She did sing in the choir, lead worship services and was actively involved with the youths as one of their biggest supporters.

At home, Devon and Shakida were noted at different times disrespecting my wife. So, I had to ask them to move out; they were already grown adults at this time, and I would not tolerate that type of behaviour. Elmarie loves children, so she was very in love with Shakida's daughter, Jazlyn.

70

One night I heard Shakida yelling at the baby as she attempted to run to Elmarie. I could see hurt and pain in my wife's eyes. I told her for peace's sake to stay away from that child.

After the one week honeymoon ended in Poconos, we had plans to continue the honeymoon for another week at Massanutten, VA. Elmarie wanted to stop by the house on our way there to see Greg. When we got to the house Greg was being taken care of by Angie and Keon (Keon was raised by Diane and I but did not want to be adopted). Angie and Keon had their stuff packed and went through the door as soon as we walked in. Thus, we could not go to Massanutten because there was no one else to take care of Greg.

That year, 2007, everything started going wrong. Elmarie quit her job and took care of Greg for a year. I had two surgeries during that time, a hernia repair, and a back surgery. Before the back surgery the doctor ordered me not to lift anything over 10 lbs. So, it fell on Elmarie to be lifting Greg in and out his chair twice per day. Unfortunately, we had to make the painful but necessary decision of putting Greg in an assisted living facility since it was too much for my wife to take care of us both. Additionally, the mortgage doubled because it was a flex arm loan instead of a locked in fixed loan. At the time, I was the sole breadwinner and what I earned was only enough to cover the bills. I remember one Sunday evening we came from church and had no dinner. Now thinking back, I see God was showing me that He chose this woman for me and that she will be always faithful.

2008 was a year characterized by increased gas prices and foreclosures. I told my wife one morning that I had made the decision to let the house foreclose because we could not afford it. I didn't know how she was going to respond, but surprisingly she stood by me. These were her words, "Babes, if you make that decision, I support you. If God wants us to live under a tree, once we are together it's fine." I was immensely relieved because here I was: just married this beautiful young woman and going through this terrible financial disaster.

We had a 2006 Burgundy Suburban that we got before our wedding. Before that we had a blue 2005 Suburban but Elmarie was not comfortable with it because Shakida would always say, "that's my mama's car." I sold it and got the new car so Elmarie would never have to hear that again. However, in 2008, with gas being over four ($4) per gallon, it was just parked. We decided to voluntarily return it to the dealer.

The house is foreclosed and we worried about where we would live. One morning while delivering newspapers, Elmarie told me to stop. She wanted to borrow somebody's Gadgette (another newspaper that we did not deliver). She got a pen and paper, and went through the classified ads. And wrote down something. She explained that she had gotten numbers to call to check out people renting their houses. I seriously doubted we could get a house without a credit check. God blessed us, she called and that evening we went to Waldorf to look at a house. It was really nice; we both liked it, but we did not have the money for the first month and the security deposit. This crushed me; I felt like a loser. But wifey comforted and encouraged me that if it is ours it will be there when God provides the money. We got the money in February; a whole two months later. We called the gentleman, and the house was still there! We knew this was God.

Elmarie went back to working at IHOP. She would help me throw newspapers then go to work 7 am to 3 pm. Things were improving; it was now time for her to go get the boys in Jamaica since their immigration process was now complete. After a three-year separation, my wife was reunited with her sons, and I was finally able to see and hold my new children.

Even before Elmarie's immigration process was final, she got her GED. She continued her studies and became a Nursing Assistant. Later, she went back and became a licensed practical nurse. Additionally, she started her BSN, but I had a stroke around that time, so she paused. I love my wife. She is very ambitious, hardworking, and always striving to make our lives better.

I remember the night that we came back from Jamaica with the boys. When we got to BWI airport, they ran over to the car. They were expecting to be driving in the Suburban, but that was not to be the case and their disappointment was written all over their faces. We were now driving a little old beat up, rusty Astro, that wifey and I hand painted white. One day Elmarie asked Oshae if he had locked the van after he got out, so people would not steal the van. His reply was, "Mom, why would anyone want to steal our car?" We all laughed uncontrollably; the car was that ugly.

Things improved but in 2010 we were still living hand to mouth. They proposed we live on the church premises since there was a house allotted for the first family. We never liked it there. It was small, and there were lots of bugs and snakes; Elmarie is terrified of snakes. We bought food and paid for the electricity while the church paid for heating oil. We stayed there for almost five years as we cleaned up our credit and saved a few dollars. The summer of 2014, we never had an air conditioner. When we asked the Chairman Trustee who was responsible for overseeing this issue he stated that some people in leadership positions are complaining that the church should not have to pay for this. Elmarie was very hurt and upset because she felt that our family was disrespected. Mama Heard found out about it, and the next day we found a new AC unit installed. She and I never had a conversation about how this happened, but wifey and I know she had something to do with it. In 2015, while going to school full time, wifey worked a full time job from 3-11 pm as a nurse's aide. We bought our first home together that year. It was nice but needed fixtures. Elmarie could be seen doing landscaping and helping with the painting etc. while still working and going to school.

After 2019, Elmarie made it known to me that she missed her family. Corona virus related deaths were rampant, and she was struggling with depression stemming from her job in the medical field. She said she wanted to relocate to RI or CT so she could be closer to family. We sold the house in MD, and bought another beautiful home in Warwick, RI. We pledge that we are going to live our best life.

CHAPTER 7
CHARGE

For those who read this book, my message to you is to trust God and never give up. No one gets the privilege of deciding on their life's package. Whatever your package is, it did not take God by surprise. The bible tells us in Jeremiah 1:5-7,

> *"Before I formed you in the womb, I knew you; before you were born, I sanctified you and ordained you a prophet to the nations. Before I formed thee in the belly, I knew thee; and before thou camest forth out of the womb I sanctified thee, and I ordained thee a prophet unto the nations. Then said I, Ah, Lord GOD! Behold, I cannot speak: for I am a child. But the LORD said unto me, Say not, I am a child: for thou shalt go to all that I shall send thee, and whatsoever I command thee thou shalt speak."*

My package came with poverty, disability, and witnessing the abuse and murder of my mother by my father. In-spite of all the negatives, the truth about me was not lost and my purpose did not go unfulfilled. God knew I was not an ordinary man. You are not ordinary. However, the 'extraordinary you' that God has already decided on, must be made manifested in your lifetime. This might not be easy, but it's not impossible. I encourage you today in this way; realize that achieving your greatest aspiration is not impossible.

The word of God according to Luke 1:37 tells us, "With God nothing is impossible". My Aunt Margaret and others doubted my ability to succeed because of my disability. But with the help of God, they have been proven wrong. There is nothing you cannot do when you put God first. Some answers come quickly while others require much patience. Never forget this truth – God knows what you can handle. It is illegal for you to give up during the race of life. You will go through many trials, tribulations and temptations, but with God your victory is guaranteed. You will have good success because the victory is already won. What is required of you, is to walk in perpetual victory.

I implore you to not disappoint your future by not showing up. Your future is saturated with wealth, abundance, peace, joy, good health and the favour of God that awaits your arrival. Please stop waiting on others to celebrate you. Begin celebrating your small and massive achievements. Never allow the negative opinions of men about you to oppress or paralyze your growth. I encourage you to not disappoint God, yourself and those who are cheering you on.

The writer of Hebrews said,

> *"wherefore seeing we also are compassed about with so great a cloud of witnesses, let us lay aside every weight, and the sin which doth so easily beset us, and let us run with patience the race that is set before us, Looking unto Jesus the author and finisher of our faith; who for the joy that was set before him endured the cross, despising the shame, and is set down at the*

right hand of the throne of God." -Hebrews 12:1-2

Is God partial? You know the answer is no. Therefore, what He has done for me, He is willing to do for you. He is the same God; He has not changed. Please be comforted in this knowledge: your situation or handicap has not rendered God powerless. The greater the odds that are against you, the greater the victorious triumph shall be. The challenges that you face are not designed to kill you, but to make you stronger and magnify the creator. No one saw it coming, but God took me From Distress to Success. Look at where He brought me – From Distress to Success.

God's blessing and protection forever be with you all.

ABOUT THE AUTHOR

Francis Joseph Ford, born in Charles County Southern Maryland, attended The Charles County public schools. As a young man, he taught Church School (Sunday School). He studied at Washington Baptist Theological Seminary, earned a BA and Master of divinity from Richmond Virginia Seminary. For seventeen (17) years he pastored one of the oldest black Baptist church in Charles county Maryland, The Mount Hope Missionary Baptist Church, located in Nanjemoy Maryland.

At the age of 74 he earned The Doctorate of Theology from Wilbur Water's Theological

Seminary. Above all the colors he loves blue, singing is his favorite hobby, next to traveling. He has a passion for giving/ helping others. Psalm 34:1, *I will bless the lord at all times, his praise shall continually be in my mouth,"* is his favorite verse from the Bible. His favorite song is," Hold to God's unchanging hands." In his leisure time he loves watching football and playing spades. He absolutely loves his family, and loves spending time with the ones he loves the most.